The Anxieties of Love

Enjoy!

Carl Cook

10/07/2020

The Anxieties of Love

Epistolary Love Poems

Carl Cook

Library of Congress Control Number:		2019916152
ISBN:	Hardcover	978-1-7960-6541-1
	Softcover	978-1-7960-6540-4
	eBook	978-1-7960-6539-8

Print information available on the last page.

Rev. date: 10/15/2019

To order additional copies of this book, contact:
Xlibris
1-888-795-4274
www.Xlibris.com
Orders@Xlibris.com
795471

What cannot letters inspire? They have souls; they can speak; they have in them all that force which expresses the transports of the heart; they have all the fire of our passions, they can raise them as much as if the persons themselves were present; they have the tenderness and delicacy of speech, and sometimes even a boldness of expression beyond it . . .

Letters were first invented for consoling such solitary wretches as myself.

—Heloise to Abelard, AD 1116

In memory of Mom and Dad

and

for my son, Rasheed

Contents

II. Falling Asleep As I Lay Next To You . . .

III. What's Most Important . . .

IV. Can Love Be Salvaged . . .

V. The Clock Ticks

VI. PS x 10

Afterword

 Foreword

1

I found these curious letters
in an antique cupboard
of cracked paint and splintered
boards, standing uprightly

in an uppermost attic. they lay under
piles of musty sweaters as if they
were respectfully kept warm from the
indifference of a hostile world.

2

Like desire, they were rather personal
and private, hidden from views
and not meant to impose on the experience
of others, like religions ought to be.

but I was curious nonetheless to read
them all and held them with
reverence, one by one, to see what insights
I would gain upon reading them.

I. What A Joy It Is To Love Again . . .

1

I'm not used to meeting strangers over
the Internet. it's a bit unsettling
revealing your private thoughts, your deepest
desires to late night phantoms staring

into a screen. I imagine it's the worst
kind of blind date—liars and
predators, self-seeking closet queens—
while the wife is half asleep.

2

You could be a serial killer or a terrorist,
a government agent spying on my
personal tastes, my antiestablishment
opinions that don't quite sit well,

or an addict to kinky sex and wacky drugs,
the kind of deviant Peeping Toms
worship through their lens or just another asshole
trying to fuck up my life once more.

1

Out of the liquid air, the phone rang.
a voice I had known before
from a distance I could not reach
wanted to express salutations

of sincerity and "just to say hello."
listening intuitively between
lines to a voice only hearts can hear,
beyond subconscious secrets.

2

Full of passion without being irrational,
you spoke like a man
of simplistic intent and made me ponder
for a while this cool facade,

those baritone words. (I've been known to
fall in love with a voice.) and since
I had met you at least once before, it was
more than your voice that moved me.

1

The photo you mailed to me
the other day sits on my
nightstand next to my bed. you seem
so sad, so thoroughly blue, I wish

I were there to kiss you, to make it
better moment for moment,
to compensate those haunting thoughts
of turning forty without a love.

2

Every morning a supplicating prayer, every
evening the same judgment, each
passing year a cruel conviction without a trial.
a life without love is anathema to bear,

and yet, as bad as it appears, it could
be worst. after all, forty years
is not eternity. at least now you can say
you'll have me to love until then . . .

1

I can tell your heart is pure,
although I've never met
you. I can hear from your brief staccato words
you're not at all like the others,

sneaking their way into my life
with poppycock and childish
games. you knew I needed more and chose
a path others had not taken.

2

I would imagine when we meet,
we'll greet each other
like a jeweler would his diamond,
critical and reverential.

with the knowledge from long years
of experience, not every precious
stone finding its way into his shop will cut
just right into a perfect little gem.

1

From the moment we spoke, everything
became a dream. reality
in its three dimensions was transfigured,
while the elements made

symbolic gestures, lending themselves
to new interpretations more
real than the elements themselves.
life was strangely new again.

2

I lost my capacity to speak, my ability
to see as a poet, unable to unearth
the perfect metaphor to clarify the sudden
fog descending, failing to grasp

the right phrase to illustrate with example
the principles of love, the feeble
communications of passion, the loud laughter of lust,
the slow transcending movement of mountains.

1

Honey locusts and swaying cattails
along a woodland pond. too
quiet like a summer evening negating
love but longing for it anyway.

your smile, not quite innocent, not quite
inviting but testing the quality of
the waters you had just stumbled upon like
a naked toe in a woodland pond.

2

I was about to ask your name until you
saw some old beloved friends and
waved to them instead. I was beginning
to get a bit curious about your

velvet lips, your fair complexion, your
tall reed like body, the way you
crossed your legs, your silver-pierced tongue,
as if I needed a subtle hint or suggestion.

1

I had no idea. like you, I thought
my chance of finding love
was lost somewhere in a fate unasked for,
buried with unalterable fortunes,

missed and retracted through
runaway opportunities, or
simply thinking naively, it'll come
if it were meant to be.

2

The distance between you and me made
us hesitant, cautious, skeptical
that all this was really happening. to think
after all these years, our prince

had truly come. to think of all the ugly
toads we had to kiss, squandering
the hours, only to realize they weren't the one.
but now, now, my love, we can awaken.

1

Over these light elusive shadows,

a chime rings restless

and indeterminate. the seasons unfold

mathematically like rhythms

of short equations, every kiss, a number.

every touch, a solution.

every thought bleeding into this physical world

informs the measurement of illusive tears.

2

What have we here but another singer,

a song worth singing to complete

the cycle? the common voice chatters

in slick vernacular, appealing

so readily to an audience of fools.

but the singer who has trained

so long for this moment commands an ovation

for a glimpse of the true.

1

Everything seems a bit less
heavier than before.
a few miles farther, the eye discovers
a broader vision beyond

the hills. our sacks are bursting
with foliage. unfamiliar
and uncertain of the landscape
the earth indeed feels good.

2

At times, the sun can be audaciously
demanding, and we must stop
for rest beside the purple waters;
look back behind the hills

and wonder how the landscape seems
to change; look farther still
and ponder if our prancing led us on
into the forest's open woods.

1

I can think of no better hour
to drink of your spirit.
to love in this moment is always
best for love. to toss

uncertain feathers against a wind,
gather the violets before
the dew has dried, a resplendent
now is the perfect hour.

2

Perhaps I will fail to set
these furies in a just
fashion or gather uprightly
such blustering clouds.

(It may sometimes prove a struggle.)
nor will you leave this
kiss to languish unluckily on crests
of lusts that do not reciprocate.

1

What a joy it is to love again
when after all these years,
I thought I never would again.
but then, by chance, so

unexpectedly, there you were,
inquiring as to who I was
and could not bring yourself nor I
to click the phone at 2:00 a.m.

2

More confident than I and overly
optimistic, you spoke
of reasons why, perhaps, you indeed
were the one for me.

me . . . reclusive and still shy at 49, stuttering
to find appropriate words
without embarrassment, careful to cover
clues of falling instantly for you.

1

Do you ever count the times
you pass in and out
of the house during these sweltering
afternoons, and leisurely,

you step onto the porch half
naked, unashamed
and fully conscious of
your intentions?

2

Exposing bare your proud
symmetric pecs,
nipples protruding like sapphires
lying across Sahara dunes

on a carefully chiseled landscape
of chocolate flesh? then
looking about to see who else
is watching besides me . . .

1

In every dream, you appear to me.
your figure hovering like
a silent sphinx of mythic wings,
lifting me above polluted

streets, ungodly gangs, psychopaths
determined to avenge the wrath
inflicted on them as toddlers, victims
whose cries were met as crimes.

2

You're wearing a leather pouch strapped to your
belted waist like a native from a jungle,
where leopards pant and wait. but you've prepared
for this peril with lethal darts, dipped

in serum designed to stop the menace
and the threat, knowing this dream
will fail if I am not straddled to your back
between your mythic wings as we lift.

1

The sheep will be sheared this spring,
their wool too warm for this
season's vernal equinox. they have not
learned to dip in ponds or find

a cozy spot beneath the dappled shade
of verdurous mulberry trees. they
prefer instead to graze all day, slowly
chewing their cud beneath the sun.

2

They gather in groups whenever they can,
wherever they find like-minded souls,
waiting without pride or anger, their fate
in the hands of the shearer who shares

their warmth with others far from these
grazing hills, and thus their joy!
not knowing for whom these blessings fall,
they love to go nude in the spring.

1

I'm in a state of disbelief. I was beginning

to believe this would never happen.

desperately seeking a soul mate God knows where,

hoping beyond hope, a final prayer.

o where is my confidante for discouraging days?

my candle lit kept burning low.

I was beginning to wonder if God's plan was

just another intimate joke on me.

2

How could I have known my love was floating

in cyberspace, drifting through

megabytes and modems of elusive memory?

one click and drag and there you were,

asking in a gentle voice, "any brothas in the room?"

impulsively, I answered, "brotha here!"

although you thought we lived too far apart,

I knew we were as close as we could get . . .

1

You came to me as a revelation,
an affirmation of a presence
undeniably within us. a light-headed
phenomenon not completely

explicable although demonstrable in a circuitous
way. intuitive preambles, soft strokes
of passionate colors, pastel whispers on a pillow,
reinventing our shared perspectives.

2

So far, I've seen your photo and heard
your voice. who could have known
technology would be our catalyst? at any rate,
I like what I see. I love what I hear,

your voice oozing like hot Southern molasses.
and when we meet, how will you respond?
with all my projected flaws exposed like an after
flood, the heart uneasy, anticipating joy.

1

I've always been unlucky in love. never quite
finding the love I craved. I've tried
everything—barhopping on weekends, cyber-
dates, personal ads, even church

functions for lonely gays. if it's true that
a good man is hard to find, believe
me, I'm a walking testament. on the other hand,
I knew it would happen one day.

2

I just didn't know when. and then it occurred
in a flash like a near-miss asteroid.
thank God, I'm in the habit of looking up.
without a doubt, I almost missed you.

I laugh now at all those lonely hours, those
empty nights with no one to hold,
where next to me lie not the man in my dreams
but that goddamn remote control!

1

You used to write me letters anonymously
and never suspected I always knew
it was you . . . so very shy, reserved, and nervous,
lacking the confidence or the balls

to ask me out, you waited much too long
before I said, "I do," to someone else.
and in retrospect, I should have confronted
your anxieties with "I know it's you . . ."

2

You could have saved me from making
the saddest mistake of my life. you
knew all along he was not for me but, out of respect,
allowed me to unravel my own misfortunes,

knowing damn well I'd learn all too soon it was you
I needed more and only you. but sometimes
fumbling about through time is the price lovers pay
before they realize who and what they truly need.

1

It's difficult to say exactly when love

has taken root, and even if

one can, such feelings are often

beyond description.

unlike a house on fire where

smoke and flames

announce disaster to the tenants

and every passerby.

2

At times, it takes a crisis of some

magnitude to magnify

the tapestry in the carpet that

somehow we could not see.

and when we do, we realize

what a bargain we paid

for such a priceless thing to

make us feel at home.

1

Whenever I reflect on the dissonance
of Schoenberg or view
the laughter embodied in Red Groom
or feel the pathos of Billy Holiday

or the irrepressible grief of Akhmatova,
I begin to see the irreplaceable
necessity of love. how could we ever think
our years have meaning without it?

2

Like cosmic phenomenon, traveling
through space is no guarantee
we will ever reach our destination,
given the fact that radiation,

magnetars, and black holes can trump
whatever preparations we made for
the journey. a dose of courage, a little prayer, and
a bit of luck can probably make it happen.

1

Into the winds, I seem to be drifting,
floating as if zero gravity
has lifted me. I see your eyes as
they pull me closer, closer . . .

I cannot pull away, nor do I wish to,
fluttering above those lashes that
never seem to blink. I feel a flush on my face
and a thumping in my heart much faster.

2

Someone or something is in charge
conducting this flight. forces
have broken free of all constraints
like a red giant before it

expands in a hot blaze, collapsing upon
itself. I may be in peril, but my
passions are in control. it would be futile
and ill-advised not to take this flight.

1

Yours indeed were the last lips I kissed.
the last taste of human musk.
the last touch tingling the granite tip,
igniting the torch consuming us

like a bonfire along the beach.
what we have is a tempest
no teapot could ever subdue like
a distant storm on Jupiter.

2

There's an openness about you I adore, a welcoming
of salubrious mercy, admissions free
for the asking. no caustic or corroding agendas,
no caveats that may prove too difficult

to digest somewhere in the near future. you
seduce and command me all at once
like Parker's omnipotent bebop, hard and fast
yet tight enough to keep me in the groove.

1

On the banks of the Schuylkill, I looked
out across the waters. a seagull
flew above my head without strain
or effort. his wings spread wide

to catch the winds that crest the river.
majestic clouds set complacent
above the skyline of Philadelphia,
not far from where you live.

2

In a moment so tranquil, in a place
transcending the malaise of city
life, the image of your being now fills me.
what an unsuspecting pleasure! I had

not known how good our God could be until
this rare unopened treasure had washed
upon my shore, and I must learn to keep it to my
heart before the tides try washing it away.

1

They seem obsessed with paltry images,
surface projections, cutie-pie values
shifting from week to week, depending
on circus trends that revolve like

fashion statements, now in, now out. avoiding
those folks who think spontaneous sex
is the catalyst to a good man's heart or that true
love begins on satin sheets is well advisable.

2

This may prove valid for a few, but for the most
part, what lies on the mirrored surface
cannot reveal the perilous risks the depths will
offer in the near or distant future.

look a little deeper, a little closer for a sense of
realness, an authenticity you won't
encounter at a gym, an aura of substance, not
likely to be found in department stores.

1

I've often dreamed of men I could have loved.
through seasons of sumptuous moonlit
nights or bitter unruly weather, the heart requires
a kindred soul to break these barren

hours. but time and hearts can be as cold as
any weather, leaving innocence exposed,
unable to battle with a child's hand the threat of
ridicule or a father's irrational punishment.

2

Could it really have been that bad? others more
capable than I can answer that question.
others now trapped in places they need not be. others
now wrapped in lies so tight they barely

breathe. others who feel betrayed, betraying others.
others depressed, confused, uneasy in their
pretending, now dream of fighting battles they should
have fought. a battle, by God, they could have won.

II. Falling Asleep As I Lay Next To You . . .

1

You approached me with sly, worrisome eyes.
your body moved with heavy thought,
giving physical hints of tantalizing moments
you had come to regret its residuals,

although you saw no reason to discontinue
what had distinguished you most,
a talent for theatrical sex, Olympic and intense,
in search of that one satisfying mate.

2

We took the time to exchange perspectives
of ourselves and of each other.
I suggested the allegorical comparison
of the tortoise and the hare.

me being, of course, the tortoise, reluctant
to stick his neck out unless necessary.
and you, with your rabbit ways, enticed me to do
just that and made me cum a little faster.

1

Tell me, why do you enjoy phone sex so
much? every time I call, you have a
desire to be seduced with vivid words of lust.
how could anyone resist a cunt like yours?

soft and velvet like mink fur, the pubes shaved
to entice and stimulate the guest
who comes to dine, immediately gratifying,
feeding the neglect of your fulfillment.

2

When distance denies our union, technology
becomes the conduit to our passions,
transporting the two of us into a semantic world
of copulating virtuosos, romantic

and salacious, imagining our bodies entwined
like two entangled contortionists,
awaiting the attention your demanding clit deserves,
"I'm ready for my close-up, Mr. De Mille."

1

The hours are eclipsed so long as you're
away. shadows are cast where no one
walks, and the entire year is like a smothering
desolation through a dismal winter.

debating whether or not our climate is changing
is no longer in dispute except for those
too dense to embrace the facts. there is still
time to reconsider unhealthy choices.

2

Time is the one thing that can never be
replaced. there are no substitutes
for what has passed. not even time machines
can fix the paradox of Grandpa's death.

and so we're left with prayers of mercy
that what is done is done to forge
a future for wiser ways, an effort to cleanse
the tainted grounds and try again.

1

I received your letter today and read
it quietly after dinner on the deck.
ducks flew in to cool themselves in the shade
on the hill beneath the pear tree.

forgive me for not paying the phone bill
on time. I'm sure it was the reason
your text could not get through and why
you felt compelled to write this letter.

2

On second thought, I'm glad the phone
was disconnected. not because I was
avoiding you but because I feel more appreciated
when you take the time and effort

to express yourself more thoughtfully
through writing as opposed to
the flippant and sometimes shallow emotions we
often share through instant technology.

1

Last night, I kissed your lips to taste
the midnight's sweet oblivion.
you showed me curves I did not know
existed. light-years away,

new stars were born, and all at once,
I understood how galaxies
evolve and why our universe, so
vast, is rapidly expanding . . .

2

Although it's true the human form
too often motivates our love,
your naked body draws me closer to
your center. the passion we share

reinforces the commitments we made,
challenging the intuitive compass
we hold to keep the needle pointing north,
to one magnetically charged direction.

1

I don't mind making love to you in the dark.
it's a lot of fun, and you know how
freaky I can get, not to mention all that kinky
stuff you do. but what I desire above

all else is to see you in the light. what
purpose does it serve to hide
the petals as they bloom or hoard the heady
nectar from the hungry butterfly?

2

Beneath the trumpet vines, you set
the garden table before lunch.
you chilled the berries and served
the honeydew sweet. you sliced

it in morsels and teased me to eat from
your hand. your half-parted lips
spoke of love and hints of lust, making
gestures of something more to come.

1

I remember that night so well. we were both in our

natural element. gently caressing the contours

of your granite legs, you lifted one gracefully toward

the heavens like the spires of a monk's cathedral.

I followed the welcoming flesh of the underside, stopping

for a moment to firmly press the extended hairy

thigh. soft bristles swirled around the entrance like angels

at the pearly gates. you shivered. you sighed . . .

2

I accepted the invitation and explored

the velvet portal. it seemed intent

on pulling in an unsuspecting finger,

clinching the knuckle to the base,

refusing to let it go. your succulent mouth

consumed the moisture from my lips,

darting a cobra-like tongue into my throat, sending signals

to explore a bit deeper, where deeper I sighed . . .

1

Falling asleep as I lay next to you is not an easy
task. you sleep nocturnally nude until
the misty dawn without cover to warm your alluring
flesh or to shield your exalted beauty.

and like a patron of the arts, I am there
to view this landscape of curvaceous
valleys and silent meadows, compelling me,
as if drug induced, to gaze and stare.

2

I'm sure you're not aware of your restless sleeping.
you twist and stretch and turn, snuggling
your derriere into my groin as if you were doing
a lap dance in your dreams, inviting me

to hold your waist, allowing my hand to follow
the curves downward where the valley
is dark and moist and sweet. but I resist the urge to act
as I respectfully acknowledge your sleep.

1

Damn, baby, those summer nights we spent together
were sizzling and salacious. I
immediately sensed your desire for discipline,
your boundless appetite for complete

surrender, demanding to tame the bitch
in the beast who never gave you
rest, cruising the avenues like an adolescent
hustler too compulsive to find peace.

2

On our very first night, your intuitions were well
tuned. you knew the image I projected
was not at all the real me and, like a genie, granted
my wishes fulfilled in long erotic sessions.

you liberated the quiet man who found
himself too often trapped in lonely
introversion. you cooed around my nipples
and offered nectar to your hummingbird.

1

Your long El Greco legs
are disproportionate
to your body. they stride
with an independence

all their own. and when you walk,
they step like rare Iberian
horses in the queen's coronation with
an inextinguishable dignity.

2

You say your tennis game
has trained them to leap
gazelle-like across the court,
agile over the turf.

I know them for the most part on
another court as they gravitate
toward angles of adagios, offering
kaleidoscopes of ecstasies.

1

Like a cumulus cloud above Montana,
your gentlemanliness attracts me.
its stillness rests against the blue, which
seems immovable, unalterable.

the valley where it hovers over
mountains are full of wild
and rapid horses who claim these pastures
as their own, their only home.

2

Someone has trampled upon your heart.
you were once free like those wild,
rampageous horses yet settled like the clouds
above Montana. the urban life,

with its carnal loves and freakish wonders,
has sucked you in, polluted
your quiet passions, altered what could
have been the only heart for me.

1

It's cool. I'm down for trying new things.
I suppose it's unrealistic to think
my sexual repertoire would satisfy every
lover I encountered. after all,

whatever you're into, however we do it,
is revealing of subconscious needs
and attitudes that might indeed test the possibility
of a future we may share together.

2

I'm not indifferent to a little pain if it brings
a little pleasure, if you know what
I mean. stuff like pinching tits, spanking ass,
deep and vigorous thrusts, you know,

shit that has you hissing and moaning for more. but
I tend to shy away from the more aggressive
acts like things that require electricity, or vinyl mats,
or rubber gloves that extend beyond the elbow.

1

I'll never understand why you wear tinted
contacts, when behind that tint
are eyes as soft and clear and natural as any
tranquil lake at the foot of mountains,

formed at a time when nature was raw
with a hushed symmetry, and you
could tell from a distant glance that
what you see is real and genuine.

2

It may be that some may need a tweak or
a lift or an art to ease projections
on the public eye. a few might require something
more radical to reconstruct what nature

has given them, but you are not one of them.
you are one of the blessed, one who can
define what beauty ought to be without commercial
fabrications or pretentious colors.

1

A million blades of grass allowed us
to love one summer afternoon
with laughter and longing and lust,
binding the two of us as we lay

naked on a landscape immaculate with
color. we stared hypnotically into
each other's eyes, unburdened by time or
crowds or a host of munching bugs.

2

I pay homage to nature's untainted
carpet of chlorophyll that blew
the blessings of clean air into our lungs
at the very moment we thought

we would hyperventilate or ejaculate
prematurely with a blast of
blushing embarrassment, but the soft emerald
landscape assured us it was quite okay.

1

I've been meaning to ask you something. why must you
always shave your pubic hairs, knowing
damn well I prefer the view au naturel? crinkled
tight curls deliberately placed exactly the way

nature intended for them to be. so why, in fact,
do you shave your hairs? does it make
your length appear a bit longer? or from that
furless anomaly, somewhat photogenic?

2

Whatever your reasons, au contraire. after all,
it's not for your sake that they're there
but maybe just for others. besides, what purpose
does it serve any of us to go through life

hairless and bald like a feline Egyptian sphinx?
think about it. the next time you feel a rush
to follow this ridiculous fashion, instead of reaching
for a razor, grab a comb or a pick or a brush.

1

Let's listen to a bit of music tonight,
some soft, relaxing melodies
to compliment our love. nothing loud
or commercially driven that young

folks are so fond of but a music we
both can embrace, a few songs
reminding us that what we share
is the light of a million stars.

2

I realize that loving me at times can be a task
when it ought to be a pleasure. no one
should be asked to adopt the faults of others, and
I'm thankful you chose to take a chance.

you could see I had some issues long buried in my
past and needed time to feel more comfortable
with the kind of love you offered. and now I can
appreciate why so many view love as magical.

1

Throughout this valley, the summer heat can be relentless

with dripping humidity, compelling us to strip

every stitch of cotton from our bodies, ensuring

the benefit of cool breezes that pass our way.

it mingles and swirl around our dangling flesh

as a respite from the heat where the musk

of vapors invites us to communicate anatomically.

our senses a calibrated map, an accurate GPS.

2

Without a word, you summoned me to your side.

our eyes locked as if in a trance, and together,

we explored our receptive bodies, inhaling natural

scents of potent stimuli to continue this

melodious probe. soft, exuberant fingers played like

a flutist on a well-tuned rod. mesmerized

and staring into those pussycat eyes, you knew I

alone would take total charge of the beast.

1

It doesn't matter what your momma
said about me or that your friends
are whispering unhealthy barbs about
where I've been and what we're

doing. people in need of love are sometimes
envious of those who are blessed
to have it. remember this when others would
have you doubt my love for you.

2

I've had my share of evening pleasures,
I'll admit to that. I've never been
sneaky or secretive and see no reason to deny
the joys of these natural delights. but

you should view this from a different perspective.
think of it as a customized apprenticeship,
prerequisites for satisfying your sweet desires before
God had worked this miracle of finding you.

1

Neurosis, dear love, is the enemy of all love.
step back for a moment and take a look.
always at the forefront of every battle, every
conflict, and every disruptive hour. be it

one or be it many, whether family or friend
or foe, be it worker or country
or culture, neurosis is a weapon of one. just one
little finger to point or stir or charge.

2

We needn't fear the variegated fog creeping
across the swamps where the crocodiles
rule. there's an antidote to every poisoned and
potentially lethal dart. there's a shield

for every spear that is thrown. but the worst
of our enemies, the greatest of all threats,
is not the boogeyman across the proverbial borders
but the affectionate psycho who lives within.

1

I think we need to be clear about what's
really going on. are the two of us
just dating, or is it something more? let's
face it, we're not two freshman in

college too naive to know the difference between
sex and love. there are times in our lives
to venture much further, beyond texting and
tweeting and laid up till dawn.

2

I've had a few lovers who were somewhat like
that. stuck at a stage when manhood for
them meant drinking and screwing for as long
as they can. they'd drive themselves

home to an empty apartment, a colorless room
somewhere in the rear, and spend
the rest of the week with friends and associates
critiquing our intimacies over the phone.

1

More likely than not, they'll take us completely
by surprise. we may find ourselves, defenses
down, attempting to converse with someone from
another galaxy, somewhere from greater

distances of the universe cosmologists had no clue.
proof of their existence no longer in question,
they may stand before us as alien automatons or some
three-legged vapor devoid of any emotions.

2

In whatever form they arrive is almost irrelevant
since the fact they are here is immediate proof
of cognitive superiority. after all, traveling this far is not
the same as Marco Polo paddling to the shores

of China. they may have just escaped the supernova
of their planet's star or decimated their global
population by depleting their natural resources, now
desperately looking to us for guidance and better ways.

1

Maybe we ought to see a medium,
a palm reader, someone
clairvoyant who could tell us for sure
this love was written above

the stars. loving you as I have,
the way I have over these
past two revealing years, has shifted
the grounds from under me.

2

I need a sense of clarity, a confirmation
dispelling intrusive doubts. the earth
is the land we walk on. the air is what we
breathe. this bed, our trust to share.

I need to know this reassuring warmth invading
me whenever I hold your hand will not cool
or crumble or carelessly creep into a distance whenever
unforeseen events attempt to undermine our love.

1

This was by choice to be a joint venture.
capital acquired through loans
of the heart and bonds of the flesh
would consolidate this deal

as any serious entrepreneur would gladly risk.
the market was just right. stock valuations
fluctuated within margins of profit, and at this
juncture, we both desperately needed it.

2

Investors are known to wager that
love is bullish where love is
new, lifting our hopes for cumulative
wealth unimagined in the past.

profits, however, may take a plunge. dips
and dives begin to take a toll. we try
like hell to adjust the inevitable. we rationalize
our losses and then sleep like bears . . .

1

Many years had passed, many empty years before
love had come my way. I rolled the dice
on countless days, but lucky in love was not to be,
although I stood my singular ground.

fake love, arbitrary, worldly, and vain, I put
aside as the last of lost causes. and any
further offers of a one-sided, self-centered love were
tossed and discarded through the opened door.

2

And now I see it was you I have waited for
all these years. for you alone, I endured
the uncertainties and the doubt, the sacrifice
of loneliness, and the wasted hours

of undeserving souls whose pitiful, ungrateful
tokens nearly broke me. but then you came
like a buoy before the years were all gone and fixed
me like a therapist for the anxieties of love.

III. What's Most Important . . .

1

I'm writing these letters for reasons
other than to express what you
already know. I've told that in so
many words before I wonder if

you're prepared to embrace this reality.
I needn't remind you how complex
and evolving our lives have become, our
thoughtless behaviors, a critical test.

2

What's most important is not always
apparent. what others are doing
sometimes prompt us to conform without
seeing where this conformity is taking us.

we could choose, the two of us, to live like
all the others, exchanging commitment
for casual encounters, failing to find what
we all seem to be looking for.

1

Appearances offer us a soothing escape, a convenient
cover for all the lies we tell each other,
especially the ones we often tell ourselves. remember
the conversation we had the other day

about health and love? I recall expressing the views
that mature love, integrated and self-assured,
is possible only when the mind and soul reflects a sense
of health, overcoming dysfunctional disorders.

2

For whatever reasons, you took this as a personal attack.
you thought I was alluding to your physical
condition, which was quite beside the point. you felt
I was abandoning our love, leaving you

to whimper like a kicked puppy or using your disability
as an excuse to rationalize a callous departure,
which, in turn, would justify your self-destructive self-pity,
which, in my view, or any other, can never be justified.

1

We see them every day. they pass
us by. they live among us—
family, friends, and neighbors,
lovers who know love only

as pain. their reservoir too empty to give.
their rivers too cluttered to receive.
emotional ties locked tight, bound by chains
in a tattered trunk of a basement.

2

When we think that love is ours,
we cannot see, for love has
no eyes to see when love is young
and has not found its center.

time, however, unravels so many things
we dare not look away. forced
to confront the truth we must own up to
and the courage to love again.

1

We may have to make a few bad choices
before we ultimately realize
the dangerous roads we must never take,
like prying open a secluded beehive

to satisfy a taste for stolen honey, only to upset
the angry residents inside, or risk a night
of spontaneous sex (sans top hat), only to awaken,
regrettably, to an excruciating morning piss.

2

Love that is foolish could lead us into a cave
where no one should explore except bats
nocturnally inclined, hanging comfortably
in a cool draft through sweltering heat.

eventually, we all learn through fault or folly
which underpass is worth the risk,
concluding some risks may be necessary if we truly
want to get to where we truly need to go . . .

1

Disasters are likely to happen, both natural
and man made, at some point in our lives.
our interior furnishings determine whether or not
we ought to build again and remove

the structures that didn't quite serve us well.
the decision is ours to reconstruct on the
very spot we condemned as hell or start all over
again, perhaps a less daunting scenario.

2

But should we choose this option, we'll have
to retrieve the old blueprints approved
and misread by some obsolete authority
and rethink the whole damn scheme;

reconsider unnecessary notions; reexamine
excessive dreams, quick fixes
that work only on Saturday nights,
and usually, my dear, not at all.

1

I need to know who and what exactly you are.

male/female? fem/butch?

top/bottom/versatile? tranny/drag/transitioning?

gay/straight/oral? lesbian/dyke?

butch queen with a twist? or leather king

into fists? am I wrong for seeking

clarity to comprehend this multitude of diversity

not fully embraced for their humanity?

2

"Dear, love, the need to know, to understand

is exactly what makes us human.

it's a first step toward knowledge and wisdom.

no need to apologize. we're here to learn.

but to answer your question in a word or two,

I am everything you are, every element and

quality exploding from a distant star, a synthesis

of evolution and the consciousness thereof."

1

All men fall short before they die.
no life can claim the absence
of fault or profess their love to be a
perfect love or deny a necessary

redemption before the grave is met.
too many awaken too late
as fools who could not see that
love is the only imperative.

2

And yet I still wonder if love is a metaphysical
entity of three-dimensional requisites
or an infantile transference from mother's
breast to yours and back to mine

or perhaps something so incontrovertibly
spiritual it defies synthetic analysis,
lest we become like Jehovah or Buddha
or Mohammed or the Christ to come.

1

Two things

can happen

between

you and I.

either this

bud will bloom

or these petals

will fall.

2

To look back now

is not to see

what we have lost but to know

what we have gained.

the difference between

heaven and hell

is the one you and

I shall make . . .

1

We met on a beach during a breezy
afternoon when sun worshippers
retreat to the casinos behind the boardwalk.
you stood on the edge of the beach,

where the chilled waters could not reach your
toes, and stared at the empty horizon as if
you were reminiscing or waiting for lost lovers
to return with renewed and fresh beginnings.

2

I can't compete with the memories of past
lovers who fulfilled your desires when
they were here. I can't erase the treasured
moments you will always cherish

and preserve. this is true for all of us. but as
you look across that great expanse,
remember that beauty lies before us and all that
settled on the beach has washed away.

1

It seems to me that knowing how to love
is to know exactly how to live. we
could spend our lives achieving many goals,
aspire to act with the noblest intent,

resolved to empower these vanishing hours.
the integrity of our existence depends on
this sacred covenant. I would not ask you to cancel any
righteous deed your maker called upon you to do.

2

Consider this: what value does it add
to these transitory days if after
all you have accomplished from these
difficult and singular endeavors,

your sacrifices were met with impersonal
applause, standing alone on a vacant
stage, abandoned by a host of lovers, unable to share
this penultimate moment with a kiss?

1

No one is safe in love. every rule
learned throughout childhood
is skewed to keep the patchwork pattern
stitched, which others, like myself,

may adore the overall intricate design,
and we ourselves appreciate
the time and extraordinary efforts it took,
sometimes heroically, to make.

2

Love may not endure, but wherever
it exists, moments of endearing
happiness compel us to try again,
to reexamine the painful

stumbling blocks within. it's not always
their fault. the choices we make
are often motivated by personal notions
unrelated to the real needs of love.

1

Before I met you, I never knew loneliness.
with deadlines and frantic appointments,
there was never enough time for serious dates,
and I considered myself a blessed

and happy man and had no reason
to doubt or dwell on all the pros
and cons of solitude or the multiple
liabilities of living alone.

2

We've been talking now for several months,
exchanging views on just about
everything, from the latest fiasco on Broadway
to the biggest mergers in corporate America.

we even wagered bets on our next presidential
candidates. but the more I get
to know you, the more I hear your gentle voice,
the more I understand what loneliness is.

1

I welcomed you from a distance I thought
you'd never travel. the doors
were kept unlocked in case I fell asleep
or if by chance you chose to arrive

before you were expected to. I've known many
to arrive too late, only to find me
waving farewell, abandoned on a lonely dock,
forsaken in the fog of a distant harbor.

2

Despite the autumn's calm, an early frost had
set in. the halls remained warm, while
the rooms were kept hospitable. I allowed you
a quiet entrance as I escorted you to the sofa.

I took your cashmere coat; you tossed your velvet
hat. you weren't at all what I expected.
dismissing doubts and reservations, we shared an
offering of the sweetest of sweet cordials.

1

If you're gonna love a man, love him all the way.
not a little bit of this or a little bit of that.
make a decision or walk away. what man wants
his happiness served on floundered dreams

or serious doubts, residuals of half love. a kiss
anointed only through lust, false touches of
intimacy, irreverent orgasms, and disruptive intercourse,
spilling seed on wrinkled sheets of sad good-byes.

2

What lover is so vain and seductively empty yet
satisfied with silly proposals, propositions
tossed on a dead-end street? true love gives more
than it could possibly take. like physics,

some proof will have to be demonstrated. our
word alone will not suffice. we might get
away with murder but not our failures to love.
it will soon stink like a forgotten corpse.

1

The rituals of love are enticing.
few can resist these realms
of anticipation. completely perplexed
as to which comes first, loves

longing or the intrusive lust. the impulse
to embrace the self-inflicted urge
or denial of one's self, rejoicing in the hour
an affirmation of the missing piece.

2

Semantics play a role, but rhetoric
cannot validate a vacant
courtship. if a lover hasn't pulled
his bucket from the well

of forgiveness, or made negotiable the vows
he promised not to compromise,
the rituals of love, so lofty when begun, dissolve
into a vacuous isle of disillusionment.

1

I sit alone in this greasy spoon,
reflecting on all the issues
we discussed as we drove into
the smog of Manhattan.

if you feel compelled to reconsider
your commitment, it can only
mean your love for me is not as certain
as you and I had thought.

2

I'm not quite sure what you really want, nor do
I think I know you well enough to say,
but somewhere, sometime ago, I've learned
that love demands a singularity, a putting

away of false hands and petty hearts, the passing
tease of carnal delights, the shame of
hidden lies, dichotomies of ambivalent vows.
love's imperial borders are nonnegotiable.

1

So what if others are spending their leisurely
hours on ephemeral diversions, casting
spiteful eyes on you as if something was wrong?
look around, wherever you go, the bars

and clubs are packed with herds of hungry whores
hopping from man to man in a desperate
quest of milking their pleasures in a throbbing
crotch of cut and uncut cock and balls.

2

Absent from these follies are a few men who'd
rather sit in a gallery and gaze upon a still life
or a portrait or a landscape, looking for clues of beauty
to comprehend their own complex reality,

or prefer instead to stay home with a good read or dance
alone to a tune that invites romance and respite
from a world of porno fantasies and pretty boys who
can only pretend to be real, authentic men.

1

Behind the big black door
flows the lilting light.
beneath the under bush
lies the fertile soil.

without this knowledge,
we may succumb.
without this courage,
defeat is ours.

2

We can always choose the easy path.
run with the crowd, wait to see.
let others march through the bitter cold.
let others risk the relentless rage.

when our neighbors preach, we ought to act.
do some good, seek what's fair.
and when the dragon blows his fiery breath,
let love be shield, let truth be sword.

1

Sometimes a lover can expect too much
as if love were an absolute fit
converging like two concentric circles,
sharing more than a common center.

when I give you time, you ask for more.
when your plate is full, you look for
seconds. and your need for sex is like a line
from *Casablanca*—"play it again, Sam."

2

Sometimes too much wood in the furnace
can overheat the house or too much
fire under the kettle can burn the beans.
every excess becomes intolerable.

even lovers have a space to respect. is it
asking too much to respect mine?
that we love each other is not the issue.
simply stated, Superman is a myth.

1

I fully understand how you feel, but wherever
you work in this world, there will be those
who present some type of challenge one way
or the other. mean-spirited, petty, neurotic,

and narcissistic people are everywhere. behaviors
unacceptable to those of us who are sane
are quite the norm for them, and learning to work
or even to live with them is not an easy task.

2

Let me give you a tip. there are three types of
people you are likely to encounter on any
given day or place: there are those who think, those
who do not think, and those who don't know

what to think. you can group these same people
as those who love, those who do not love,
and those who don't know how to love. and there
you have it, the tragic history of our world.

1

We sat in a room together listening to raindrops
dancing on the roof, although too dark
to see the willow swaying its branches like Nubian
women swimming naked on the coast of Africa.

the rain danced all night like a chorus line
on Broadway, tap-tapping heels with
a synchronized joint consciousness, as we held
each other mutually, metaphysically.

2

Here we embraced a truth no other truth can
substitute or fabricate or adjudicate
in any court of law. as natural as a river flowing
toward the sea, we moved as one, kneeling

before an altar so plain and humble many will
overlook because their provincial views
have been distorted by the narrow regulations
established by a posse of conformists.

1

All kinds are out there to steal your love—
the magicians, flim flams, robbers, and
actors. the selfish, the actress, the pretentious,
the fool. the confused, contrite, contrary,

and cunning, prowling like jackals
on the Kalahari Desert, crouched
in ambush for this year's meal, an exquisite
cuisine for these gourmet thieves.

2

It's tempting to shut down, lock your heart
in a silver box and view *"this bitter earth"*
through squinted eyes of regret and remorse,
convinced all love is out to hurt, hurling

your spirit toward shackles of shame, trapped
in bondage not easily escaped except
through wages too high to pay. but pay you must
or view this life from the dirt of a ditch.

1

Do not take love too seriously.
love was never meant to be
a sturdy rope tossed into uncertain seas
to drowning men who cannot

find their way. such love can bring us down,
down beneath the quagmire of psychic
pits, where distinctions are not made between
a mother's love and a lover's love.

2

All men need love though some
can live without it, and most
will live a lifetime unaware of how
it peels away logistically

the segments of their lives like the quaint
and quartered art of origami.
so much like jazz, so much to improvise.
sometimes blue. sometimes cool.

IV. Can Love Be Salvaged . . .

1

Love is not easy. it never is.

its force reverberates

like the shifting plates beneath the earth,

sometimes catastrophically,

rearranging the windows in the upper room

where the view of the horizon

is not what we thought it was. a casual stroll

cannot be taken for granted.

2

What then do we do when the house has fallen?

personal treasures crumbling

beneath the crying weight of brick

and stone and mortar?

can love be salvaged? rescued

like a dazed toddler pulled

naked from the rubble? and when to assume

from the aftershock our love is lost?

1

When I was a boy, the pastor delivered
a sermon one Sunday afternoon.
the sanctuary was flush in sunlight pouring
its reverence through stained glass

windows. the topic that afternoon was "walking
through valleys." and in his humble way,
he began by saying, "if you haven't reached
your sunless valley yet, one day you will."

2

I was far too young to understand the gravity of
his words or the somber tone in his booming
voice. he delivered that sermon like the terrifying
lightning of a thunder storm, his feet stomping

the pulpit like an angry Zeus on his throne . . . and now
that I have grown into my own manhood as
a father and as a lover, it seems I spend more time
than I care to admit "walking through valleys."

1

By the time you read this letter, its message
may be obsolete. ignore your fears
of the irrational, be they friend or family
or foe. whatever gifts the heavens

have granted, embrace them. swing the bat
as if it were your last strike. nothing
can substitute what a billion years of natural
selection was meant for you to give.

2

It may not appear to be a blessing when
others are plotting plausible plans
to harass and vex you into denial, shame,
and psychic mutilation. if love is

theirs to give, you need not worry. only the shameless
will kick a heart around. be forever mindful.
there's only one way to please the gods and that's
to share your gift as if it were a treasury of gold.

1

Anger is sometimes unavoidable when things
go awry in relationships. no one
wants to be played like a rag doll tossed
in a rancid box, tied with ribbons

and bows of lies. the first law of love
is respect (ask Aretha), and
the second is equally important,
uncompromising sincerity.

2

A recourse to counseling can serve to check
the anger from explosive displays,
and essential to everyone, forgiveness is the final
but difficult path to redemption. it's up

to you to find that path. it's okay to ask for assistance.
you may indeed find that path much sooner.
of course, this is not to say every couple can be saved
or even to suggest every scoundrel ought to be.

1

The way things are going, we'll look back years
from now at our desolate and depleted
planet and wonder how we managed to deceive
ourselves so convincingly about our

vital resources. looking up into gray skies,
we'll wonder where all the precious blue
has gone, now saturated with carbonize crystals
too lethal to allow love to flourish.

2

Extravagance, ignorance, the vanities of the ego,
our thoughtless herd psychology,
our thirst for political lies, religious hypocrisy
feeding the dreams of the dispossessed;

gadgets and gizmos demanding more time
than babies in their cribs; our support
of political fools who fail to lift the people
out from the gravities of the past.

1

It's not always a sure thing, and that's what
makes it so scary. regardless how often
we "fall in love," each time is qualitatively and
quantifiably different. even if you were the last

in a line of great Casanovas, or unlucky enough
to have married nine times, or was known
as the pimp daddy of the world, you would never
be able to master the details of this art.

2

It sometimes feel as if we're being rushed
into surgery. cut open like festive pigs
for the holidays, exposing all our vital loins
to inhospitable procedures, callous

hands snatching out the more tender parts
and bagging them for sale on the open
market. then escorted back to our private rooms
feeling more dazed and more vulnerable.

1

I envy those who have found true love. it's
more rare than most would ever care to
admit. I've had my share of casual encounters
like spontaneous sex on a long-term basis,

yet all the while, I continued to look for someone
with a deeper connection, attempting to erase
those stubborn doubts that seem to linger long after
the expensive honeymoon we both regret.

2

You wanted a convenient companionship, someone
to release you from your loneliness. I can
relate having experienced that emptiness myself.
but I needed something more, much more.

something like a wish-fulfilling dream, a promise
kept like fresh cut flowers left on the afternoon
doorstep. the problem was, all you wanted was a
boyfriend, but what I needed was a husband.

1

Stand firm, my brothers! be the man
your heart and soul must will.
whatever love I show for you or you
for me, together or alone in our

private space, or out in public, lovingly.
as soldiers at the front or voices in
a choir, never to doubt what we already
know . . . blessed is the love we share.

2

Tell no lies to disgrace the heart! commit
no vows entrenched in fear! decide
your life as your only life! guide your love
through every battlefield! and when

the wicked foreboding mouths are shut, while
the stars still burn above our kiss,
forgive the ignorant who tormented us as the
price we endured for a certified love.

1

One of the worst things you can do
is to keep a secret from
your lover. it all comes out sooner
or later, and when it does,

the fallout can be greater than
a catastrophic accident
at a nuclear power plant. it may take
years before anyone can recover.

2

As your partner, I deserve to know
the truth. to lift the public
veil that everyone else is acquainted
with, a public persona whose

purpose it is to impress or to flatter
or to cover some incriminating
stain you've lost the guts to discuss with
the only one who truly matters.

1

Everyone was curious about this particular man—
middle-aged, slightly bald, professional
in his work and demeanor, twice divorced,
two kids in college, and a car.

true love had seemed to elude him. hidden
behind the mask was a man few of us
had met, by invitation only, and somehow
in his pursuit of success, he had not lived.

2

His cock was thick and imposing like a
pit bull from the ghetto, displayed
aggressively through tight denim jeans. the thought
of holding it had a dangerous appeal.

at forty-five, he was still finding himself,
dreamed of husky men and lusty lads,
and found the courage from a buddy to release
the longing that had locked him in.

1

Your wife drove up to the door without
expression or even so much as a
smile of anticipation as you got in. she
seemed to have looked the other

way as if she did not care. you acted the role
of faithful husband and did well
to hide your deepest concerns. you pulled it
altogether as if nothing was wrong.

2

I love it when a circus comes to town.
I love everything about it.
the animals marching in single file,
the death-defying feats,

the clowns who make us laugh.
I love the big-top tents and
the smell of disheveled hay, but I never
wanted to run away to join one.

1

Behind every foreboding cloud, the sun shines
luminous. we needn't sulk when blue skies
appear ominous and gray. darkness may linger
for a while but not forever unless, of course,

we have some reason to think it will like an asteroid
wandering into our cosmic neighborhood,
plundering our magnetosphere like a vile, lascivious
rapist the innocence of a pubescent girl.

2

If things are going well with you, don't second-guess reality.
most of what we consider our
liabilities are seldom asked for. too much analysis
can spoil a treasured masterpiece with fingerprints

from our own unhealthy cooking. should
blessings come your way, embrace them.
though not as a burdened student in Bible class but
rather as a physician who finds his patient well.

1

They warned me before I met you.
they said offensive things about
you I won't repeat or pretend I was
ready to believe. so I kept my

distance reluctantly, unsure if the risk
of loving you was worth
the taking, unsure if a man's reputation
is as certain as his reality.

2

In many ways, you confirmed what they
were saying. you drank too much and
popped a few pills on top of that. then fell
asleep at the moment we could have

fucked (typical addict). but because I dug a bit
deeper, I found the man behind the booze
and wagered your recovery could lift you out of
the muck and into redemptive love.

1

That you find yourself behind bars again
does not surprise me. it's become
the metaphor you won't let go, excusing
yourself and hiding behind social

and genetic presuppositions, which all of us
are subjected to. but instead of grace,
you look for pity when indeed prayers
and confessions are well in order.

2

Until you can reflect and trace the acts
that brought you here, until you
can declare the liquid paths you walked,
until your views expand beyond

the distance between your eyes, your
motives less selfish, surrendering
to the source from whence all love flows,
such bars will keep you here forever.

1

I can't even imagine going to jail. my
claustrophobia simply could not
endure it. I may as well pack my bags
and walk straight to hell.

you've been there before, your foolish
and thoughtless behaviors got
you there, so stripping down and spreading
your cheeks is no big deal for you.

2

I don't mean to make light of your situation.
serving time is serious business. your
freedom, your love, your friends, your family,
your livelihood, all lost in an instant.

now what have you to learn? what morsel of
meaning can you share from this? it's one
thing to be punished for the principles of your soul.
it's quite another for just being an asshole.

1

We were in denial for so long
we barely gave it a thought
that beneath our fake macho exteriors,
we could, in fact, be lovers.

we married as an extension of this
cover-up and became "swingers"
as an excuse to come together, to share
what we truly desired, each other.

2

Finally, we corralled enough courage
to confess to ourselves and
then to each other and, lastly, to our wives
and children, who would never again

see us as the men they thought we were.
and although we rejoiced in
a hard-fought freedom, we had to admit
what a fuckup it had all become.

1

You can't trust envious people who conspire.
their poison is more lethal than snake
spit. when they love but cannot have, beware!
they hide their fatal fangs in wounded

passions, spinning devious plans to punish
the innocent perpetrator, guilty only of
being the object of their love. but revenge they must get
to silence the molten anger gurgling in their breasts.

2

Unrequited love can trigger rage from another
era, like an infant who needs
its mother's tit. the same is true of men as
well as women. these bitches have

no gender. like Satan in hell, it's a state of mind.
unhappy and frustrated, they find justice
in casting spells like evil witches, transmuting their
incompleteness into unsavory, ugly toads.

1

When you think of it, we both could
have had love. we could have
had each other. like a salmon in heat ready
to spawn, I would have gladly swum

upstream, dodging bear claws and jagged-edge
rocks, dangerously shallow waters, oblivious
to a certified mortality. anointed by your sensuous
hands, I would welcome a resting peace.

2

Your focus was sadly misplaced. committed
to a lackluster job, cliquish friends,
and empty promises, you chose to pass
me by and lost the one blessed thing

that could nurture growth, split wide
the reluctant heart, and fortify
the soul, leaving me hopeless, like
a helpless salmon, asking why.

1

I gave you too much credit for your scarlet smile.
your wide searchlight eyes looking
for something other than love. I surrendered
to love's allure, but subconsciously,

I was suspicious. what I felt more deeply denied
reality. I pretended your kisses were
warm and intimate. I allowed myself the luxury
of illusion. I made myself a victim.

2

Hidden agendas may get you through the door,
even through the bedroom door, perhaps
even the jangling change of a well-worn wallet.
but take note! traps are set and laid

unsuspectingly throughout the corridors of love.
we don't intentionally do it, but our
doubts demand it. the heart must find redemption
and the grin on the fox's face erased.

1

Softly with resolve, let's meet again in a forest

of dream like meadows, where lovers

meander under the welcoming arms of

the oldest pines to refresh our love.

no one will ever know or even care to look

where only true love can walk on a

path reserved for them. the foolish, the impulsive

can never find us in our special place.

2

Love ought to be organic, spontaneous,

natural like the ecological balance

we find across our elliptical universe. a few

surprises may be necessary to keep

us alert but never to take these moments

for granted like the young so often do.

besides, what do they know? except the instant

gratification of a thoughtless screw?

We waited quite some time for this autumn meeting.
neither of us were willing to compromise
what we knew we both deserved and desired
and unwilling to trade our dragon lilies

for lowly thistles. the weeds are always plentiful.
rain is all they need to instigate their
rapid growth, hampering our efforts to cultivate
a gathering of exquisite summer roses.

2

May this blessing rest on your sweet,
endearing lips, affirming each
kiss with wonderment, convinced
of miracles and God's unending

grace. o, love, sing to me now with
supple and soothing voice.
whatever lyrics you choose, every vowel
expressed is a song I anticipate.

1

I've cleared all the weeds and dead
foliage before winter was upon
us, trimmed the vines, cut the hedges
on both sides, and kept the

height low enough to say good morning.
I spaced the irises to spread across
the fence more evenly and fed our gorgeous
willow a healthy dose of fresh compost.

2

These efforts are absolutely necessary,
lest we take our gardens for granted
and risk losing the natural order of things.
like love, neglect can throw a garden

into total disarray. unwanted growth, invasive
vines and shrubbery, poison ivy,
skunks, possums, and moles can drive
the finest of constant gardeners mad.

1

"There are laws that govern our universe,"
systems and matters that coexist
within idioms and principles, studied
and tested by those so equipped to

do so. and we are part of those systems,
responding and reacting very much in
the same manners our molecules and atoms
do but with greater consequence.

2

You might see it a bit differently, but we
may, in fact, agree on the same
suppositions. so why are we arguing,
raising hell and launching emotive

fire balls meant to weaken the very link that
makes us strong? science, again,
is needed for clarity. it attempts to explain
the thermodynamics of love.

1

I don't live in a temporal world,
nor do I wish to love there.
what good is love if love is a passing
fling, something you

pick up on Friday, only to discard
before the next new work week begins,
like an old bill you forgot to pay?

2

Why is it so many make such a
big deal about fucking? not
intimate, personal lovemaking but just
fucking as if some psycho social

antidote were grafted onto their genitals?
if this is what you're looking
for, pass me by. save the bullshit
for the next Ms. Lewinsky.

V. The Clock Ticks

1

The thoughts we think swim like fish
in a pond. and when we pull them
from the waters, the words we use to describe
these fish are no more certain or still

than the waters. this could explain why so
much of what we say of love is never
quite adequate, only the approximate mark
of what we think we felt or thought.

2

There's a lot of double-talk when it comes
to expressing our deepest emotions,
clearly because most of us will only dive so deep
to retrieve them. self-analysis is not an easy

task. and listening to family or friends or fools
when it comes to consulting love might
simply add to all the drama and confusion. talk to
the spirit within, cut out the middleman.

1

Cosmologists have a way of cooking up
theories before all the ingredients
are brought to the kitchen. dinner is not
complete until Momma has served

the apple pie. and you can't be certain of
the recipe until you've served and
shared your dish with someone who knows
a little something about good cooking.

2

Another perspective will correct us if we're
wrong. even Einstein needs a Hawking.
and the dish we serve as poets will not always
taste as yummy as it looks. only the reader

can determine if what we say is elegant or true.
love can sometimes feel like cacti when
handled improperly, and seeing is not always believing,
which is why fools fall erratically in love.

1

Wouldn't it be marvelous if we could
all fall in love with the ideal
embedded in our heads? like Pygmalion,
sculpt a peerless beauty whose

charms were designed to meet our specific
needs, waiting patiently for the goddess
Aphrodite to melt the marble and free the spirit
embodied in the silence of dead stone.

2

Such things exist only in wish-fulfilling dreams
or tales from Greek mythology. quite
naturally, we'll always idealize the object of our
love, which may explain why sex is so

explosive in the beginning. experience plays the greater
role in testing the authenticity of these initial
exchanges, deciding the difference between a genuine
intimacy and the irrational illusions of lust.

1

Someone told me years ago that a good lover

is like a big old easy chair you just can't

live without, too comfortable to throw away and

too much a part of the decor that may

prove disorienting by changing or shuffling

the furniture around at this late date. why

would anyone risk losing something of value

that's been proven to work all these years?

2

Fools do it all the time. breakups and divorces are

as common as hangovers, mostly by lovers who

haven't learned to adjust their disruptive hang-ups

or even to realize what those hang-ups are.

much of it begins in early childhood like parents who

fight and argue in front of toddlers. I don't want

this to ever happen to us. I just wanna be your big old

easy chair you'll never find reason to throw out.

1

The clock ticks whether or not
we love or die, and what
was set into motion many years ago
will not make a difference

in the quality of love or the psychic battles
waged in its name. even if you decide
love is not yours to give in this brief moment,
now is all the time we have to give.

2

Torrential downpours are always possible,
problems persisting in spite of
progress aggressively pursued. there are
limits to time. limits to how long

love can find assurance, the confidence
to acknowledge the approaching
storm, the courage to speak as a child without
pretense, without the ruination of regret.

1

Sometimes love is a disappointment.
sometimes living can be hell.
sometimes the life we choose is obstructed
by realities beyond our control.

sometimes pain is quite necessary.
sometimes crying is inevitable.
sometimes what we anticipate are shadows
from someone else's dream.

2

Deceit does not win the war, although
it sometimes wins the battle.
and greed is often cloaked as progress
on the site where cancers grow.

if we could only embrace what's everlasting
and nurture our heavenly grace,
we would triumph over every earthly evil
until it rots in an unmarked grave.

1

The grave is the last party we shall ever
have to attend. however shamefully
shy or gregarious our friends found us to be,
we'll all be there, dressed in fashions

that seem never out of style. a style no one cares
to imitate or stake claims of originality but,
for good or bad, reluctantly accepts the invitation
with a wink of a teary eye.

2

A sudden or tragic loss can mask the fact that
every sorrow is a passing one. and every
joy, however small, strengthens through eternity.
the presence of his highness may be hidden

from the sweltering mass of a weeping crowd.
excessive gestures, rituals that feign
to heal, expressions of self-pity all contribute to an
atmosphere that clouds the love that links us all.

1

I used to die but not no more. I used to leave
the house without ever looking up
or around or ever wondered what the hell
was it all about but not no more.

I had a way of blocking the view, ignoring
everything that didn't quite have
something to do with me. I was good at that,
good at not seeing what I needed to see.

2

I used to die so uneventfully, a slow, obnoxious death.
I'd shine my coffin almost every day, equipped
with the latest gizmos and bling—cell phones, titanium
rings, and digital TVs. until, of course, I met you.

you, who kissed in whispering breaths, raised me out of
a mass grave and peeled the copper pennies from
my shuttered eyes. you made me see what I needed to see.
your love brought life, and light, and death no more.

1

Toward the end of summer, we had a chance
to exchange our views on death. after all,
we won't be here forever, although like many,
we wish we could. but nevertheless, plans

will have to be made, and leaving it up to our
children may not always prove the best
idea, no matter how well-meaning they are.
death does not always bring out the best.

2

As we spoke, you seem preoccupied, a bit
anxious about the role death may play
in reclaiming our souls, our spirits, the force of
love that moved and protected us in life.

call it whatever you will. if God can hold the
entire universe in his hands—every
element, every molecule, every atom—then surely
he can hold our sacred love as well.

1

Sartre may have been mistaken.
there is always an exit,
but only those who think it
through will ever come

to finding it. every element changes
when conditions allow it to.
even black holes are escapable if
we can find the hidden portals.

2

Sometimes we have to readjust
the possibilities. like a Rubik's
Cube, twist and turn until a match
is made. if you surrender too

soon, you'll find victory was assured
in one more move. I haven't
given up on you yet. and we have
every reason to try again.

1

I had doubts I would ever see you again.
no sweet seraphic chords were
heard as we dined for lunch for a casual
date at the renovated Heritage.

your eyes were quick but accurate
as you scanned my khaki
pants, looking for something more limber
like the supple notes of a clarinet.

2

I've come to learn not every gardener
will choose a birch to grace
his landscape. many prefer the massive
arms of a shady sycamore.

whatever your taste, my dear,
I'll say this about you:
your thick, imposing frame has sprung
the steeplejack in me.

1

Let's keep in touch by writing letters. let's not
forget or offend we are here. we could
easily ignore the fact we are brothers now,
although at times, we tried to be lovers.

some things, I suppose, may never come to pass,
like trying to fit incongruent pieces into
a puzzle. you'll only succeed in wasting more time
as if any of us had any more time to waste.

2

I know how important money is to you. I know how
calculating you are when counting your pennies.
it's not a bad thing to work hard for your wealth, but at what
price will you sacrifice others? this may have

created a vacuum where the void should have been
filled with love. and I have no doubt you still do.
but if you measure your life by mutual funds, dollar for
dollar, cent for cent, o, what a poor life you've lived.

1

Having given it some thought,
I've come to realize you
indeed were the one for me, but
at the time, I wasn't quite

sure. I had a few reservations that I informed
you of . . . if only we had waited a little
longer, allowed the seed to root, the bud to
fully bloom, the storm to wash over us.

2

Remembrance is no substitute
for what we could have had.
past memories can lend a smile but
cannot reinstate a bungled

opportunity. I have myself to blame.
all that is left is a vision
of your beauty, your long El Greco legs
reclining in the nude.

1

Marriage remains sacred
for quite a few of us.
if we meddle or tempt
the lover from

his covenant, who
is to blame?
surely not the vows
we pledged.

2

If you offer,
should I accept?
if you give,
shall I take?

if the jackal is thirsty,
away from home,
should he drink from
another water hole?

1

There's an intruder somewhere in this house,
our home of love. strange, though, it is.
it was never planned or intended, yet we
found ourselves together serving

laughter and drinks, hors d'oeuvres, and
exchanging political views. and then
he excused himself to use our bathroom in the
master bedroom, inspecting how we slept.

2

How could we have known when the guests
arrived, our eggs would crack and
break, only to discover (almost too late)
we stood in the mix of an omelet?

but what other options (we considered)
did we have? chase the fucker out
with a butcher knife? or swallow this
impending omelet whole?

1

Was it me? or was it you?
I don't quite know
who plucked the petals
from the well-worn

rose and threw them fiercely
into an angry wind.
maybe it was the two of us.
we can only look within.

2

God alone loves with a perfect love,
neither of us can claim. but if we
stand courageous against the wrongs
determined to rearrange

our fate and renounce the viperous
passions betraying us at every
turn, we earn a simple but lasting grace:
to ask forgiveness or to give it.

1

Like a sorcerer's apprentice,
I wish I could sweep away
this mess you and I have made.
but like every child,

innocent and unaware of most
things, we must learn
to clean this muddle ourselves.
no one else will do.

2

Love will prove not so difficult
to mend if the two involved
have made an honest pact to do so.
only one, however, is needed

to obstruct the possible growth
of fresh foliage or trample
underfoot the little sprouts that
had just begun to grow.

1

An ugly disposition does not become you,
nor does it prove anything significantly
worthy, let alone how tough you can be. who
gives a damn if you growl and snarl,

attempting to intimidate men of character whom
you've misjudged as being weak, when, in
fact, it is them from whom you must learn to climb
a mountain with a steady and fearless integrity?

2

Your only power lies in getting others
to do your bidding, and these are
usually the dunces who think their shadows
are assassins out to get them. I pity

your sad dilemma. your world is rarely filled
with love or beauty. happiness for you
is to see others suffer because their suffering
distracts you from reflecting on your own.

1

You thought by having a child, we
could salvage this reckless
relationship as if a dinghy attached
could save a ship from sinking.

you thought if you could lose yourself
in a child's cry or hold its
precious hand, our love would grow
despite enormous odds against.

2

You were mistaken again. our conflicting
views of what is real and what is
worthy continue to be at odds. I reject
love's distorted urge to be a victim

and long ago have cast out demons
feeding on adolescent dreams
of love being less than liberating work,
a mutual consensus of two.

1

I know I sometimes sound a bit mushy
and sentimental, but to see you
happy is all that I desire. to hold
the wrinkles of discontent at

bay with the sweetest of kisses, knowing
the world does not change or
turn for love. we are in command only when
the soul is allowed to illuminate.

2

These are not easy times. courage is
a premium too many have
decided they can't afford. yet without it,
all that we hope for, aspire to,

and cherish is wasted along the promenades
of profit. love is bartered like trinkets
at a carnival, exchanging our inner soul
for the latest fad or fading fashion.

1

We can make this happen as we dreamed
it could always be, the right fit
in the right hour, our desires answered
like a well-planned meal, assuaging

our hunger. you need this as much as I,
and denials will only serve to make
a mockery of the time we spent searching
and waiting, wishing and longing.

2

It seems to me love is like the lottery. we're
lucky if we can find the perfect
combination to hit the big one. the odds are
a million to one, if not more. so many

appear to be distracted or complacent or immersed
in their own personal agendas like
bits of drama that drag and drain the soul, too
helpless to learn, too hopeless to love.

1

I spotted a clever snake in my garden
the other day. it was neither long
nor menacing, thick nor threatening,
but like every garden snake,

he was quick to squirm his slender
body into one of many holes
he had managed to bore among
the marigolds and wisteria.

2

And when I saw him slithering away, he
seemed neither here nor there
but purposely went about his business
drilling more unwelcome tunnels

on the very spot I had planned an array
of arresting beauty. and then
I paused and thought a while. he made me think
of what your love has meant to me.

VI. PS x 10

1

Did our president attempt a chance at treason?
will Caesar have his way to haunt our
great democracy with wicked Trojan horse ideas?
ideas inspiring political loathing and

misguided misogynistic lust? history disputes this as
antithetical to what our founding fathers taught.
or does he think (or can he think?) these wicked leanings
could soon replace what "We the People" have built?

2

Putin winks with a broad smile when referring
to his irascible 45. "I wonder
how deep his throat would stretch if I made
him my personal bitch. after all,

Russia could expand remarkably fast if I took
his throat and his ass! we both are two of a
kind, you know. the kind of men who would pimp
their mothers just for one more pile of dough."

1

It's much too late for whispers now. we all were

witnesses and knew exactly what was

happening and cannot lie or fake an ignorance

of the matter. with pleasant smiles and

vocal silence, we became certified accomplices,

de facto spies too cowardly to break ranks

or to tell what we had seen. we held to mafia values,

preferring destruction than necessity to reform.

2

Perhaps one day we'll stand as real men

and real women ought—men who

do not quake when power takes the upper

hand and women unafraid to rewrite

the script as it was given, bowing to no authority

or social norms that cast a spiteful eye.

we can't afford to take these matters lightly!

our survival, our democracy is at stake!

1

The spirit of my mother spoke to me,
saying, "son, I am here where
theories do not exist. where the church
cannot install its pews or paint

our minds with symbolic language as a
trade-off for more substantive things.
I am here scattered in the nebula where
lovers converge to form new stars."

2

"You were right after all. I needn't fear
the final journey of my life. what
I was taught never came to pass and was
glad I spent so many days in my

garden and so many nights looking up. I'm
happy we shared those conversations
together. I understand now how science and
math define the substance of love."

1

The quest for love may sometimes prove

in vain. such hopes can

vanquish with the aging years, leaving

passions long extinguished

with the last forgotten kiss. too embarrassed

to remember, too beleaguered to confess.

unfaltering faith keeps vigil through the valley,

patient like a rare Brazilian orchid.

2

It may take time to reinforce the calm among the

madness, knowing that hearts do not always

seek to heal, transcending the angst of personal pain

and the disillusion of disappointing lovers.

love can only go so far to relieve our losses. it

was never meant to be salvation for all

the battles fought within. never meant to mitigate

every sorrow, every sickness, every sin.

1

Society points a wicked finger and tells you

who and what you are and where

exactly you should go. they give you a name,

a number, and a group to join. and it's

not a request or a polite invitation but a mandate

they expect you to oblige. it's all promoted

through parents, and publications, and TV stories

without so much of a whisper, "your choice."

2

And believe it or not, most people buy into it. it's

easier that way. after all, when you think

of it, what purpose does it serve to rewrap

the package, or rewrite the formula, or

even to risk your precious life just to say "it ain't so!"

look what happened to Socrates and Jesus,

to Gandhi and King. all died like St. Joan and Sir Raleigh

giving hypocrites the boot to their ugly lies.

1

Every pleasure is addictive regardless.
be it power or sex or cigarettes
or drugs or drink or food or money
or gold or treasure or porn or

vaping, shopping and hoarding stuff for which we have
no need or exaggerated religiosity and all
those other compulsive disorders like excessive
hand washing or the vanities of the mirror.

2

And there's another component to addictions,
one that encompasses the two of us.
it's not easy to explain because the emotions
are somehow buried in the context of our

subconscious, revealed only when they surface
in our interactions with each other like my
compulsion to yell at you, and instead of taking your
rightful stand, you bow your head and cry.

1

O, love, there is no greater depth of sorrow,
no wound that cuts so wide or pain
so everlasting or inconceivably unbearable
as that as the sudden death of a child.

no matter if mine or yours or theirs or where
or how it came to be, we drink our tears
and drain ourselves of all but grief as seconds pass
as slow as all eternity, where Jesus wept.

2

How do we forgive our fortunes when fate has
faltered to a halt? what comfort could
we offer to souls so far removed from their
own blessings, detached from what they

had come to think was theirs, now lost to delirious
lamentations, locked within dimensions
where time and time alone can lead us back
to an ever-present responsive love?

1

The last time I saw him, he was just hanging
there, unmoved and unnerved like
the full moon above him. I stepped a little
closer to get a clearer view, a better

glance to see what they had done. more than
anyone, he was my dearest friend, and it
saddened me to realize I may never see him
again, just hanging there, left for dead.

2

In many ways, this was a sorrowful day for
lovers everywhere. to see his eyes fixed
upward, his arms bound to the ends of wood
as if he were calling us back into the fold.

he was a good man who didn't deserve the treatment
they inflicted, but I will always remember
him as a brother who loved us all and, in so doing,
taught us all how to love one another.

1

Within this quiet room, under these quiet stars,

the violence of this world must pass. we

long for a shared community, our neighbors affirmed

in truth, with love, in peace, with compassion.

desires of this world can sing a lustful tune to

negate and deny our distinctive humanity,

allowing the fickleness of fools to feed on weapons

as they slaughter the innocence of children.

2

O save us, dear Lord, in these precious hours!

protect us as we strive to love as you

command in justice and integrity. and should

we find ourselves confused or in conflict,

tempted and tainted like lost supplicants without a soul,

O guide us, dear Lord! keep us as we were,

molded in grace, and make us altogether whole again

within this quiet room, under these quiet stars . . . amen.

Afterword

1

Looking back now on my living,
I can see more clearly
the rough-hewn pattern I have woven,
born of needs extending beyond

temporal claims. the risk of not knowing
what I should have known;
the necessary fumbling we all encounter,
embarrassment, delay, the uninvited.

2

Somewhere in this diversified forest,
I have found redemption.
in spite of fallen trees, above the boulders,
someone shoved onto my path,

despite the darkness that is always there
and the stillness that does not move.
I give an offering to this wondrous forest and beat
a path where the darkness cannot follow.